TH

COTSWOLD RING

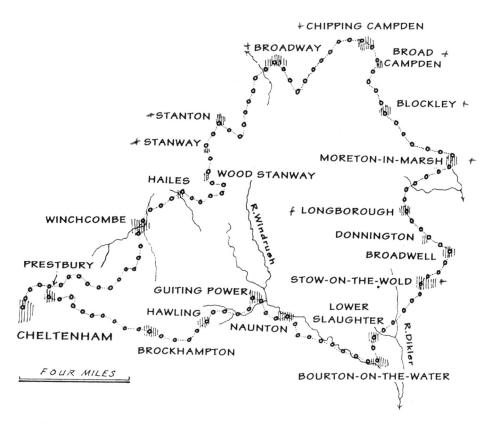

CHIPPING CAMPDEN

BROADWAY

BROAD CAMPDEN

BLOCKLEY

STANTON

STANWAY

MORETON-IN-MARSH

HAILES

WOOD STANWAY

R.Windrush

WINCHCOMBE

LONGBOROUGH

DONNINGTON

BROADWELL

PRESTBURY

STOW-ON-THE-WOLD

GUITING POWER

LOWER SLAUGHTER

HAWLING

NAUNTON

R.Dikler

CHELTENHAM

BROCKHAMPTON

BOURTON-ON-THE-WATER

FOUR MILES

1

Published by
REARDON & SON
Publishers
56 Upper Norwood Street, Leckhampton
Cheltenham, Glos, GL53 ODU

Cover illustration
Peter T Reardon

ISBN 1-873877-16-1

Maps
Mark Richards

Layout & Design
Nicholas Reardon

Printed
in
Cheltenham, England

THE
COTSWOLD RING

INTRODUCTION

The Cotswold Ring is an original route designed by Cotswold Walking Holidays Ltd. to take in much of the best of the northern Cotswolds. The aim is to provide contrast, interest and variety, making use of existing rights of way and long distance footpaths to create a satisfying circular route. A total of 55 miles in length, it can be undertaken over the course of a week (or less), or in sections. To that end a list of taxi companies with their telephone numbers has been included.

Cotswold Walking Holidays are able to organise accommodation and transportation of luggage. For further information telephone or fax: (01242) 254353.   We hope that you enjoy the walk and the Cotswolds - please do not hesitate to let us know how we can improve this walk.

THE ROUTE AND ITS PATHS. The route of the Cotswold Ring to some extent uses existing long distance footpaths. Thus, as well as the conventional right-of-way signs (yellow arrow for a footpath, blue arrow for a bridleway which is open to horse riders as well as walkers), you will also come across other indicators:

The Cotswold Way - a white dot

The Heart of England Way - an oak tree

The Windrush Way - a disc, half green, half white

The Wardens Way - a W in white and green

Should any of these paths be obstructed, please let us know.

Itinerary

Day 1. Walk Cheltenham to Winchcombe.
Day 2. Walk Winchcombe to Broadway.
Day 3. Walk Broadway to Chipping Campden.
Day 4. Walk Chipping Campden to Moreton-in-Marsh.
Day 5. Walk Moreton to Bourton-on-the-Water.
Day 6. Walk Bourton to Cheltenham.

Maps

We hope that the hand drawn maps in this booklet, combined with the detailed text, are sufficient for your needs. However, if you need further assistance, the following maps are recommended:

OS Landranger maps 150, 151, 163
OS Pathfinder maps 1066, 1067, 1043, 1044, 1068
OS Leisure map, Cotswolds

LUNCH PLANNER

Day 1: By starting at 0900 you should arrive in Winchcombe in time for a late lunch. Otherwise arrange to purchase sandwiches the night before.
Day 2: Lunch in Stanton is possible at the Mount Inn if you arrive before 2PM (usually marginal, especially if you visit Hailes Abbey). Hayles Fruit Farm (just beyond Hailes Abbey) has a tea room. There is a tea room on the main road just before Stanway.
Day 3: You should arrive in Chipping Campden in good time to find pubs etc all open.
Day 4: In Blockley there is a pub (the Crown) or Lady Northwick 's Tea Room selling snacks and excellent home made cakes.
Day 5: The Fox at Broadwell serves good food. Stow has a large number of inns and restaurants.
Day 6: In Naunton the Black Horse (opening at 12) serves excellent lunches. Your timing, however, is likely to take you to the Farmers Arms in Guiting Power.

TAXI COMPANIES

Here are some telephone numbers that may be useful:
Taxis (Cheltenham):
Astra Cabs. Tel: 01242 252233
A 2 B Cabs. Tel: 01242 580580
Associated Taxis: 01242 523523

Barry's Taxis, Moreton in Marsh. Tel: 01608 650876
Limozena, Bourton-on-the-Water. Tel: 01451 820972
David Prout, Bourton-on-the-Water. Tel: 01451 821478
Cotswold Elite Taxis, Blockley. Tel: 01386 593561
Mobile: 0378 914685

THE ROUTE

These instructions are designed to be as detailed as possible. On the whole the paths are well signposted but on occasion landmarks are difficult to locate. If you find the instructions confusing at any point, it is recommended that you look for the next landmark mentioned in the text (village, church etc) and simply head for it following your nose. For example, Day 2, the descent from Stumps Cross to Wood Stanway - this is difficult to describe in a way that makes sense to everyone, so try to identify the route in advance. We hope, however, that the text is clear - any suggestions are welcome.

Please remember to shut all gates behind you! Bon voyage!

DISTANCES

DISTANCES ARE IN MILES.
1 MILE = 1.61 kms.
1 YARD = 0.91 METRES.

Day 1 - Cheltenham to Winchcombe.

Time: 4 - 4.5 hours.
Distance: 8.5 miles.

It is suggested that you begin your walk at the beautiful Pittville Pump Rooms in Pittville Park in the northern part of Cheltenham. Look at the Pittville Pump Rooms with the park behind you and take the road to the RIGHT (Eastern Approach Drive).

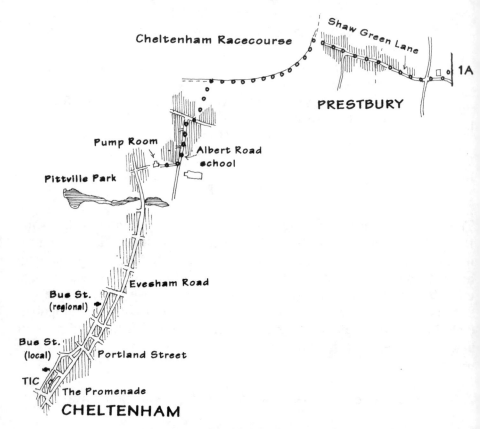

At the end turn LEFT into ALBERT ROAD, and then RIGHT along NEWBARN LANE. After a few yards look for a footpath on the LEFT. Take this and keep going until you come to a stile at a large open area close to the horse racecourse. Go straight ahead to the edge of the racecourse and turn RIGHT. Follow a path as it follows the racecourse on the left. Houses will close in from the right and eventually you will come to a footbridge on the LEFT, to cross a small stream.

Cross this and then turn RIGHT to continue along the path. After a while (about 400 yards), just after a metal stile, you will come to a small field. Here, bear DIAGONALLY RIGHT to the TOP RIGHT CORNER. Then pass through to a road, lined with houses. Go straight ahead until you come to a junction (this is PRESTBURY, England's most haunted village).

Cross over to enter SHAW GREEN LANE. In front and above you is Cleeve Hill (the highest point in the Cotswolds!) which you are about to climb, using the cluster of three radio masts as a landmark. Continue to the main road. Cross into GRAVEL PIT LANE.

Pass the rubbish disposal site and turn immediately LEFT along a lane. At a corner where the road goes right, CROSS A STILE IN FRONT OF YOU into a field. Cross this to another stile and enter another field. Turn RIGHT and head fo another stile/gate into another field. This long, uneven field rises up gradually - keep to the LEFT side, alongside woodland, eventually looking for a stile in the TOP LEFT HAND CORNER.

Cross this and then bear LEFT and continue the climb, soon bearing a little RIGHT to head for a stile/gate at the edge of some trees. Go over and then cross a small clearing, looking for a path rising up through woods. This emerges onto an area of comparatively flat grassland, with a wall in front of you beyond the bushes.

Turn a LITTLE LEFT and walk for 150 yards approximately to look for a stile in the wall. Cross this onto Cleeve Common and turn sharp RIGHT to follow the edge of the common with that same wall now on your right. Continue towards the radio masts.

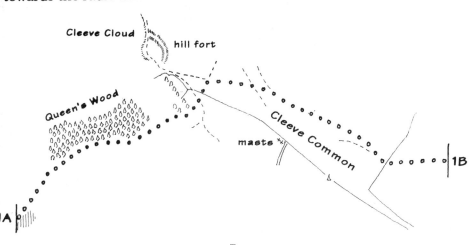

As you approach the masts, start to ease away to the LEFT, taking a DIAGONAL line. There is no landmark here but walk among the bushes for 700 yards approximately as the common dips down to a wall where you should look for a stile/gate (possibly marked with an ARROW with a WHITE DOT which signifies the COTSWOLD WAY, a long distance footpath you follow with some variations as far as Chipping Campden).

This takes you onto a track which runs by the side of a field. Follow this track down to deserted WONTLEY FARM. After the gate turn LEFT and follow this as it curves, rises and then straightens out.

Keep going along a track until you meet a sign on the right for BELAS KNAP. Turn RIGHT, following the left edge of the field until, eventually, you come to a stile. This brings you to Belas Knap, an ancient long barrow or burial chamber. Signs here offer a historical insight into what is one of the most perfect examples of its kind in the country.

Pass in front of the barrow and leave the enclosure by means of a stone stile, opposite the one by which you entered. This takes you onto a path. Turn LEFT and immediately go through a kissing gate. Then turn RIGHT and quickly LEFT. You are walking along the edge of a field, with woodland beyond a wall on the right. Continue along here, among a few trees and bushes, watching out for stones and roots sticking out of the ground. Emerge from the trees, pass a gate on the right (enjoying views of Winchcombe), until you come to another kissing gate on the RIGHT.

Go through to descend a field at its right hand margin. Follow it as it curves left at the bottom, with woodland on the right, until you meet a steep little dip. Turn RIGHT here through a kissing gate to descend sharply amid trees to a road (CORNDEAN LANE).

Turn RIGHT here (good views ahead to Winchcombe and Sudeley Castle) and follow the road WITH CARE (some traffic passes along here). After about 500 yards a track will appear on the LEFT. Take this to pass Humblebee Cottages on the right and then, after a curving descent, a farm on the left. Enter a narrow defile between hedge and metal railings (with the beautiful Wadfield Farmhouse behind you on the left and Sudeley Castle below you) and descend the field. Cross a stile and keep to the right margin of the next field as it curves left and flattens out. Then look for a stile on the RIGHT.

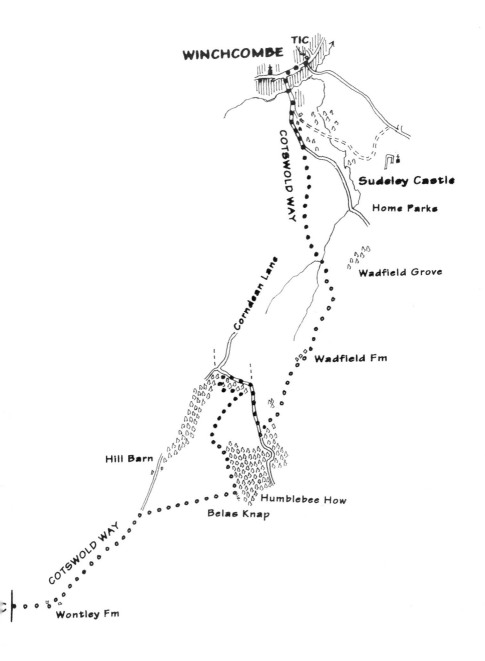

WINCHCOMBE

TIC

COTSWOLD WAY

Sudeley Castle

Home Parks

Corndean Lane

Wadfield Grove

Wadfield Fm

Hill Barn

Humblebee How

Belas Knap

COTSWOLD WAY

Wontley Fm

Cross this into a field and turn immediately LEFT. Follow this to the next corner; turn RIGHT and immediately look LEFT to go down a few steps to a footbridge. Cross this to a field. Cross this on a diagonal line following the obvious path in the general direction of Winchcombe church tower. This will bring you to another field which you cross in much the same way; and then another which again you cross on the same line until you come to a gate at a road.

Turn LEFT and follow this road as it passes the entrance to Sudeley Castle (take note of the opening hours if you want to return after you have checked into your hotel), bears left, crosses a bridge and rises up VINEYARD STREET to the centre of Winchcombe.

At the junction the church and Railway Museum are to your left. By turning right you will pass the Plaisterers Arms and eventually come to the Tourist Information Centre on the left.

Day 2 - Winchcombe to Broadway.

Time: by leaving at 0930, with a visit to Hailes Abbey, you are likely to arrive in Broadway 1600/1630.
Distance: 10.5 miles.

Walk northeast along the main street away from the church and leave the town. Where the pavement runs out you will come to a road on the right. Ignore this - the turning you want is NEXT right (PUCK PIT LANE), just after the next house. FOR SAFETY'S SAKE, HOWEVER, CROSS THE ROAD TO USE THE PAVEMENT ON THE LEFT AND THEN RECROSS INTO PUCK PIT LANE.

Walk along Puck Pit Lane (the old pilgrim route to Hailes Abbey). After some while this will come to an end at a stile. Cross this into a field. Head across this, bearing a LITTLE LEFT - if an old barn is still standing, you may use this as a landmark. Then cross into another field (although there is no real hedge or wall to separate them) and head straight across this to a kissing gate. Go through and head for another gate. Go through into another field and head across it diagonally. At the other side of the field turn RIGHT along the field's left margin until you come to a track.

Turn LEFT along this and follow it to a road. At the road (watch out for traffic) turn RIGHT and then, quite soon, turn LEFT, alongside houses. Quite soon go through a gate into a field. Cross this, with the ruins of Hailes Abbey to the right, to another road. Turn RIGHT here (although you may like to visit the fascinating little church in front of you) and pass the entrance to Hailes Abbey on the right. A visit to this is recommended and be sure to use the cassette commentary included in the price of the ticket.

The walk continues along this road. Where it turns right to the fruit farm and tea room CUT OFF ALONG A RISING STONY TRACK AMID TREES. This rises for quite some time. When it eventually leaves the woods behind, look for a stile on the LEFT leading into a meadow. Cross this and look for another stile or gate into another meadow.

Head for the TOP RIGHT CORNER where a steep dirt path takes you up to the RIGHT (ignore other arrows telling you to go left) to a point among the trees (BECKBURY CAMP) where there is a stone monument which apparently marks the spot where Thomas Cromwell watched Hailes Abbey burn in 1539, part of Henry VIII's dissolution of the monasteries.

Enter the neighbouring field and keep to the left hand margin, with views to left, as it passes through the ramparts of an Iron Age fort. Pass into a second field. At the corner DO NOT CONTINUE INTO THE WOODS but follow the field as it curves RIGHT and after a short while look for a track on the LEFT.

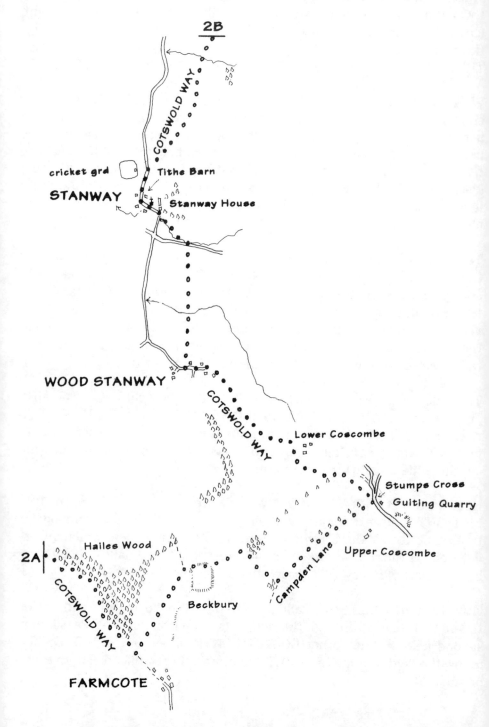

Follow this and almost immediately, bear LEFT at another track. Follow this down all the way (you can see a quarry in the distance ahead of you), passing through a gate and then by a row of trees, to a road at STUMPS CROSS.

At the road turn LEFT and then immediately LEFT again (almost back on yourself) over a stile onto a scrubby path with dense woodland below you to the right.

Wonderful views will soon greet you if the weather is decent. Keep to the path as it curves left and then TAKE CARE - the path is not obvious, for you must soon descend the slope on the right on a diagonal line (look for arrows). Follow this down to a stile into a field and turn RIGHT.

Continue down to pass a house (with stables and swimming pool) on the right and look for a stile on the RIGHT. Cross into a field and turn LEFT to make a short, sharp descent past a tree. Then turn LEFT via a stile or gate into another field. Cross this, curving just a little right, to enter the next field. Then bear RIGHT to descend diagonally to the bottom where a gate leads onto a track towards Glebe Farm.

Pass through the farmyard with its barking dogs to enter the village of Wood Stanway. Pass several attractive houses and then, 150 yards approximately after the farm, look for a footpath on the RIGHT. Take this and pass through a gate into a field and continue across fields on the same line until you come to a BUSY ROAD.

Cross WITH CARE to the other side. Turn LEFT along the pavement (tea rooms may be open ahead of you; a public telephone is along the road behind you) and then turn almost immediately RIGHT over a stile/gate into a meadow and orchard. Head across this for 100 yards to look for a wooden kissing gate with carved swan's head. Go straight ahead, with the walls of Stanway House on the right to pass a cottage on the left and arrive at a road.

Turn RIGHT towards the magnificent 17th century gatehouse to Stanway House. This gatehouse was designed by a local mason, Timothy Strong. The house, still owned and occupied by Lord Neidpath, dates back to 1000 years when it was owned by Tewkesbury Abbey.

Keep to the road (beware of traffic) as it goes left and right. It passes tennis courts, left, then another entrance to Stanway, right (note the magnificent

14th century Tithe Barn), and the cricket pitch, left, with the pavilion donated by J.M. Barrie (author of Peter Pan). Then look for railings on the RIGHT with a stile - cross this and walk a few yards to another. Cross this and enter a huge estate meadow. Keep on a diagonal line to cross an avenue of trees and keep on the same line to look for a stile beyond a magnificent copper beech.

Cross the stile and, keeping more or less on the same line, walk across a succession of fields to Stanton. The last field will bring you to railings at the edge of Stanton. Cross onto a lane and turn LEFT. This will bring you to a junction. Turn RIGHT to walk through the village of Stanton, preserved unspoilt since the 1920s when the architect Sir Philip Stott bought and restored it. Note the absence of yellow lines, telegraph poles etc. - it is frequently used for period television productions.

Walk through to where the road curves left; do not follow it but bear RIGHT to continue up the village as far as the WAR MEMORIAL on the left. (If you have reached this point by 1.45PM, you will have time to obtain lunch at the MOUNT INN up the hill at the end of the street). There is also a public telephone up here. IF NOT GOING to the pub turn left by the memorial and head for the church, leaving the Cotswold Way. Turn into the churchyard. Keep RIGHT of the church and turn RIGHT along an alleyway to a stile. Cross into a field.

Go straight across this field to a stile and go over into another field. You are now to stay on this line (with a little variation here and there), about half way up the slope, all the way to Buckland, parallel with the road below you to the left. In the process you will pass the village of LAVERTON below you and eventually pass the Buckland Manor Hotel on the left. Immediately after this cut left to find your way onto the road that leads into Buckland.

Pass the church on the left and continue until a footpath appears on the RIGHT between the beautiful old rectory (the oldest working rectory in the county) and some cottages.

Follow this into a sloping meadow and head for a stile.Cross this, then another, and continue ahead, creeping up towards the tree line on the right. Where the trees end a stile will take you into another meadow. Head straight across towards a bridle gate at the edge of woodland.

14

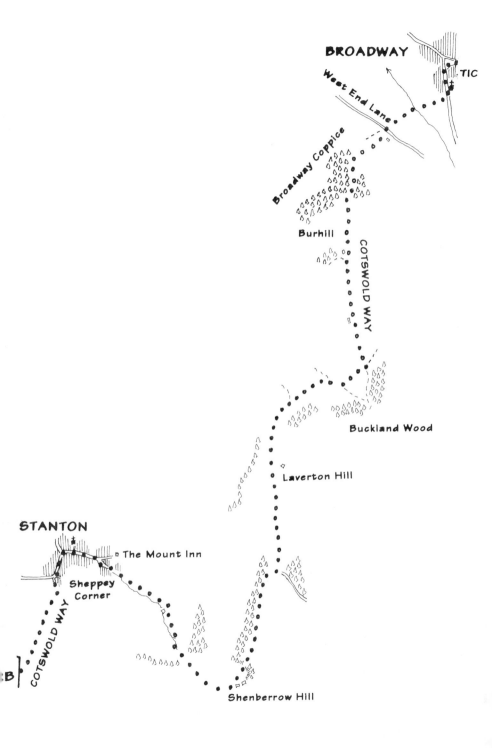

BROADWAY

TIC

West End Lane

Broadway Coppice

Burhill

COTSWOLD WAY

Buckland Wood

Laverton Hill

STANTON

The Mount Inn

Sheppey
Corner

COTSWOLD WAY

B

Shenberrow Hill

Enter a path. Continue straight for a short while and then follow this as it curves right through bushes. Eventually enter woodland proper and continue STRAIGHT ON to a stile at the edge of a field, with Broadway below you.

You are heading in the direction of the church. Descend this field to look for a stile AT A ROAD IN THE BOTTOM RIGHT HAND CORNER. Cross this road (West End Lane) to enter another field. Keep going in the direction of the church and at the road turn LEFT. Pass the church and continue to a junction in the heart of Broadway.

Day 3: Broadway to Chipping Campden.

Time: Including a visit to Broadway Tower, approx. 3 hours.
Distance: 4.5 miles.

Today is the shortest walk but first you must climb to Broadway Tower! Walk up through Broadway in the direction of the hills.

Continue for some time - pass the Stratford road on the left, and then, after about 200 yards, look for a SIGNPOSTED FOOTPATH ON THE RIGHT. Pass along a track by houses. Enter a field and continue straight for a short while, crossing stiles/gates as you go. Shortly begin to curve LEFT up the slope in the direction of Broadway Tower, as you rejoin the Cotswold Way.

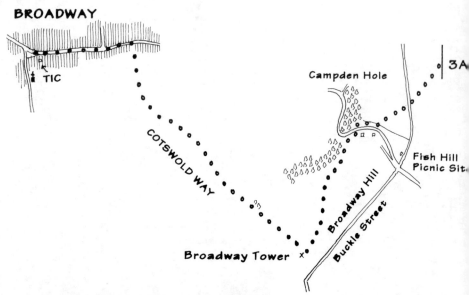

This long climb takes you up the left side of several fields and eventually brings you to a turnstile by BROADWAY TOWER, on your right. (If you wish to go in you may enter to buy a ticket and then return through the turnstile to continue the walk).

If NOT visiting the tower turn LEFT at the turnstile and then walk along the ridge. Enter the next field and follow the path along a gully. This will eventually lead to the edge of woodland. Enter this, continue straight ahead more or less to the other side of the woods (ignoring the track on the right, which is not a right of way) and then follow arrows on trees to bear RIGHT around the edge of the woods to join the track. Almost immediately look for a path on the LEFT through the grass to meet the main road at Fish Hill. CROSS THIS WITH GREAT CARE. GO ONLY WHEN NO TRAFFIC IS VISIBLE IN EITHER DIRECTION.

On the other side of a road look for a path which bears RIGHTISH. Follow it for a few yards and then bear LEFT and follow the path as it curves right before looking for a stile on the LEFT which leads into a field. Cross this to the other side and a road. Cross the road and enter the field on the other side.

Cross this diagonally to enter another field and cross this on the same line. Then, on the RIGHT look for a stile onto a broad swathe of grass (THE MILE DRIVE). Once on this just keep on for about half a mile, until it ends. Then continue on the same line by jinking LEFT along a defile and then RIGHT to walk along the left side of a field, alongside the road on the left.

As you near the end of the field, you should be able to cut away to the right diagonally and join a road leading into Chipping Campden (if there is no path through the crop just follow the contour of the field as it bears right at the corner).

Continue down this road. Just after a cottage and a shallow left bend, look for a footpath on the LEFT. Enter a field, and then bear immediately RIGHT to cross diagonally to the far corner by houses. Walk along a path between houses, cross a road, walk between more houses and at the next road turn RIGHT to walk into Chipping Campden.

Ahead of you is the Volunteer (serving excellent food).

Turn LEFT at the junction and walk into the centre of Chipping Campden. Whilst you are in Chipping Campden you may like to visit the church, the museum, the Ernest Wilson Remembrance Garden, and the silversmith workshop. Or you may like to walk up Dover's Hill, scene of the annual Cotswold Olympiks.

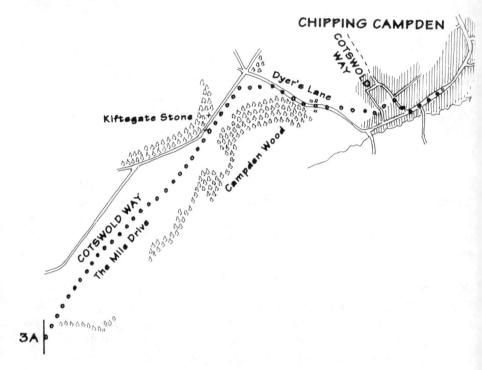

Day 4: Chipping Campden to Moreton-in-Marsh

Time about 1.75 - 2 hours to Blockley. Then 2 - 2.5 hours to Moreton. Distance: 8 miles

Pass beneath the arch to the left of the Noel Arms Hotel (as you look at it) and continue through the car park. Walk straight on along a road which eventually dwindles to a path.

Pass a sports ground and then, where the path meets a road, turn LEFT into a field and then immediately RIGHT to follow the right hand margin of the field. Carry straight on, eventually walking up the slope of the field ahead of you (good views of Chipping Campden behind you). Where the path divides, bear RIGHTISH towards a house amid trees.

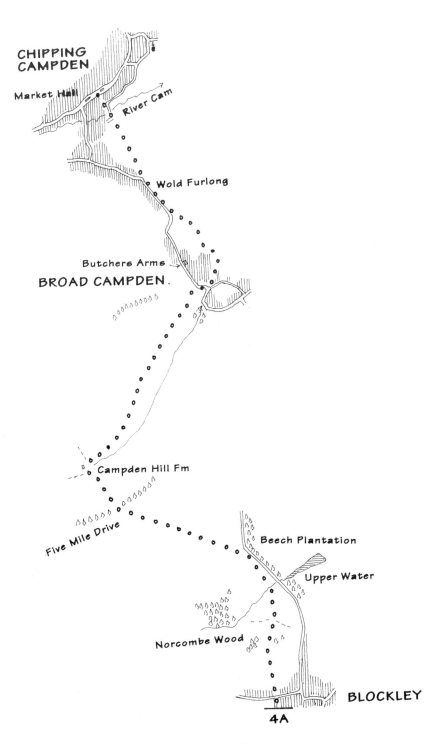

CHIPPING
CAMPDEN

Market Hall

River Cam

Wold Furlong

Butchers Arms

BROAD CAMPDEN.

Campden Hill Fm

Five Mile Drive

Beech Plantation

Upper Water

Norcombe Wood

BLOCKLEY

4A

19

Pass through a stile/gate and walk along the drive in front of the house. Towards the end of the house cut away LEFTISH from the drive to a gate which will take you into an alley of Broad Campden.

Follow this to pass the old (Quaker) Friends Meeting House on the left and then to emerge onto the green near the church. Go straight down to the road and turn RIGHT. The road bends right towards a pub. Just about opposite the pub go through a gate into a field with a wall/buildings on the left.
(You are now following the HEART of ENGLAND WAY, intermittently marked by the symbol of an oak tree, which links Campden with Bourton).

Keep left to follow the path beneath the trees and as the field opens up on the left continue straight ahead to find a gate/stile in the hedge on the other side of the field.

Go through into another field and then bear RIGHTISH on a diagonal to the top right corner and pass into another field (although there is no dividing hedge or wall). Continue to where there is an overgrown patch enclosed by metal fencing on the right. Pass below this and then immediately after turn sharp RIGHT up the slope to the top of the ridge.

At the top turn LEFT and walk along the ridge passing stiles and brambles as you go. Once again there are good views behind you. This path comes to an end above a farmhouse. Bear LEFT to descend past the farmhouse on the right, and a pond on your left, until you meet a gate/stile at a track. Turn LEFT and follow this clear track as it bears right and then straightens out to climb gently towards trees.

Keep to the same track to pass through the trees and over the ridge. Descend to a point where the track goes left to a farm. At this point carry straight by leaving the track to descend through bushes. A road will appear below you to the left but you turn RIGHT into a field and then immediately LEFT.

Descend to the valley bottom, passing through gates where they arise. At the bottom pass into another field and then climb up the other side, bearing a LITTLE RIGHT to some trees at the top. Pass beneath the trees to go straight across to the other side of the field in front of you. Then turn RIGHT and look for a stile on your LEFT. Go over this and pass through a few trees into a field. Go straight across this towards the houses of BLOCKLEY.

Look for a stile to take you between houses to the road. Cross this to enter another minor road. Where this emerges at the village green turn LEFT to descend into the village. At the junction you may turn right for the Crown pub; or turn left towards the church where you will find Lady Northwick 's Tea Rooms, which serves excellent homemade cakes. There are also public lavatories close to the church.

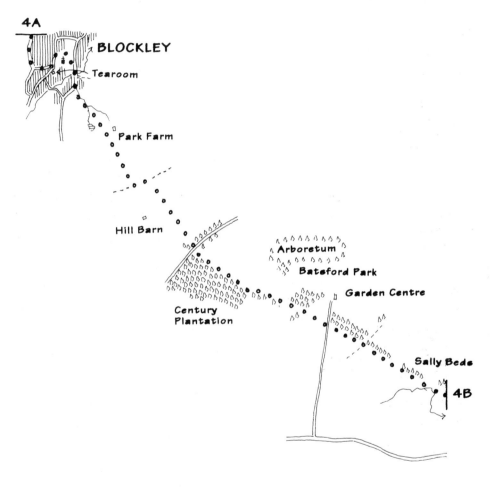

The route proceeds from the church. Pass through the churchyard, with the church itself on the right. Leave the churchyard on the other side and then turn sharp RIGHT down a steepish lane to the main road.

At the road turn RIGHT and follow the road as it passes a B & B on the left. The road curves left, passes a lane on the left, and just where it curves right look for a track on the LEFT, known as The Duck Paddle.

Enter a field and, keeping to its left margin, continue to a stile/gate to enter the next field. Here bear RIGHTISH to go up the field diagonally to pass below a house. Soon after look for a stile at the corner of another field in front of you. Cross this stile, enter the field and turn LEFT to climb the field to the TOP LEFT HAND CORNER (with fine views behind you).

At the top go through a gate/stile and turn LEFT amid trees. Continue for a few yards, pass through a gate/stile and turn RIGHT through another gate/stile to walk along the right margin of a field, with hedge on your right. Continue on this line to a road.

Cross over to enter a track among trees (part of Batsford Arboretum). Continue through the trees as the track descends and narrows to a perhaps fairly overgrown path. Where this ends by a gateway on the left, bear RIGHT for a few yards to a wider track. Turn LEFT and continue the descent.

Then, after about 300 yards, where the track continues descending to the left, LEAVE THE TRACK TO GO STRAIGHT AHEAD ALONG A SHORT, GRASSY PATH. This will bring you to a field in front of you. Go straight across this to a track. Cross the track (the entrance to Batsford) to enter another field to the right of a house.

Cross this ribbed field heading for a gate/stile in the left corner. Go through this and enter another field - now keep on this same line (keeping to the left hand side of the fields), crossing stiles where they arise. In the last field the houses of Moreton will appear - head for these, passing more or less along the middle of the field, looking for a path that runs between the houses, to the right of garden plots.

This will cross a road and then bring you to the centre of Moreton.

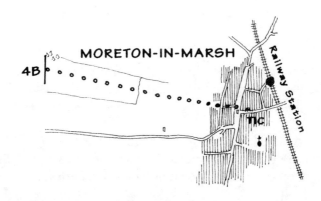

Day 5: Moreton to Bourton-on-the-Water.

Time: By leaving at 0930, you should arrive at Bourton in mid afternoon.
Distance: 12 miles.

Walk south along the main street which runs along the old Roman road known as the Fosse Way. As you approach the end of the town look for PARKERS LANE on the RIGHT, by a large pond. Go down here to pass the fire station on the left and continue to the bottom.

Follow the path as it bears LEFT (do not go into the field in front of you) and keep to the path until you come to a gate at a field.

Cross the field to enter another field. Keep to the right hand margin and follow the path as it turns RIGHT.

Still keep to the right hand margin of this field and the one following. Then, in the third field, keep straight but drift a LITTLE TO THE LEFT to enter another field in front of you. Follow its left hand margin and on the other side enter yet another field with an area of woodland in front of you. Bear RIGHT here to cross the field through a row of stunted trees and head for the right hand corner of the woodland. Go LEFT around the corner of the woods, and where you meet a track across the field turn RIGHT along it to head for a farm.

Keep just left of Upper Rye Farm and follow the track beyond it as it follows the right margin of the field. The track then curves LEFT and then RIGHT through a gateway to gradually ascend the slope ahead. Just after the Keepers Cottage on the right turn LEFT (no arrows or marks here, so be careful) to walk along the right hand margin of a field towards a gate.

(If instead of turning left, you turn right into a field, you can see the magnificent facade of Sezincote House on the left after about 200 yards, a rare example outside India of Mogul architecture).

Go through the gate into another field where you will find yourself on the left hand margin. Keep on the same line to eventually pass LONGBOROUGH church on the left and then to come to a road in the heart of the village.

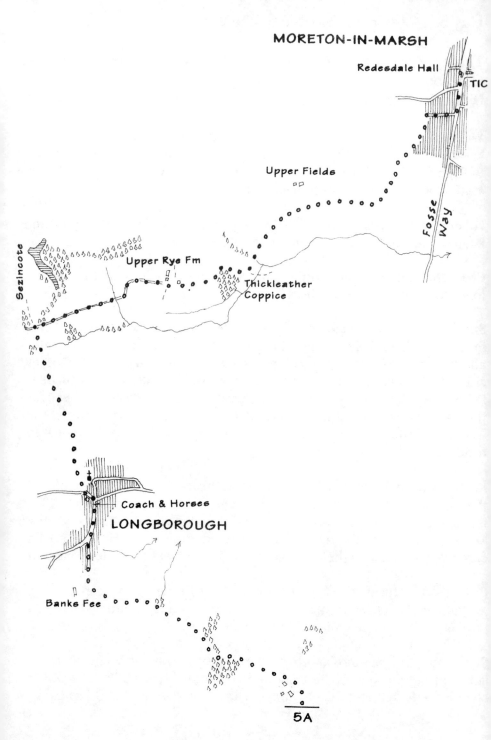

MORETON-IN-MARSH

Redesdale Hall

TIC

Upper Fields

Fosse Way

Sezincote

Upper Rye Fm

Thickleather
Coppice

Coach & Horses

LONGBOROUGH

Banks Fee

5A

24

Turn LEFT and then bear RIGHT past the pub. Within a few yards you will come to a road on the RIGHT. Take this and continue to where this divides.

At that point take the LOWER NARROWER ROAD going LEFTISH past a water spout and carry straight on. This is LOVE WALK. Go almost to the end. A footpath sign will probably appear on the left - ignore that and walk a few yards further on where a stone stile is embedded in the wall on the LEFT.

Cross this into a rough field and take a diagonal line to head for the TOP RIGHT HAND CORNER. Go through a gate and turn LEFT onto a track that will go through the woods. Follow this until, where it curves away to the left, you CARRY STRAIGHT ON to follow the right hand margin of a field. This will ascend gently to a brambly path. Take this as it curves left around the girth of the hill to come to a gate/stile at the edge of a meadow.

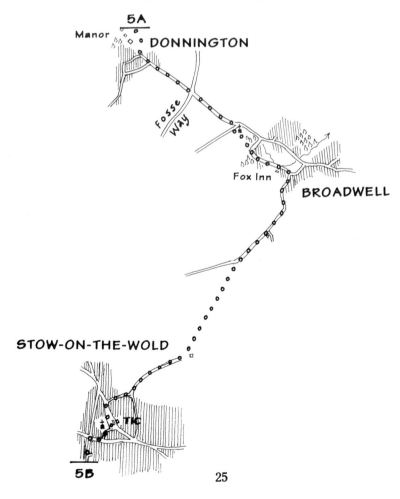

Go across this, bearing RIGHTISH to go over the slant of the slope to arrive at a stile/gate at a farm on the edge of DONNINGTON. Go over this and continue through the farmyard, soon turning LEFT and then RIGHT to come to another stile/gate at a field.

Enter the field and follow the curve of the ha-ha in front of Donnington Manor as it bears right. This will bring you to a gate/stile at a road.

Turn LEFT and carry straight on, ignoring another road on the right, until you come to the BUSY MAIN ROAD. Cross this WITH GREAT CARE and follow the road opposite to the village of BROADWELL.

As you approach the village the church appears on the RIGHT - pass through the churchyard (well known for its bale tombstones) and then continue straight across the grass, passing the handsome stone house on the right. Carry straight on and you will eventually arrive at the huge village green and the pub, the Fox Inn. You are now about half an hour from Stow.

Continue past the pub until you come to a road on the RIGHT. Take this as it curves and ascends - about half a mile outside Broadwell, where the slope begins to level out at a corner, look for a tree lined path on the LEFT.

Take this and continue as it eventually becomes a track by a house, dipping and curving past the wells that were Stow's sole water supply until the late 19th century. The track comes to an end at a road on the edge of Stow. Turn RIGHT and follow the road as it curves LEFT into the square of STOW-on-the-WOLD.

Leave the square at the corner nearest the church and follow the lane to the road. At the road turn RIGHT and at the traffic lights turn LEFT onto the Bourton road, using the pavement on the left hand side.

Follow this down for about a quarter of a mile, looking for a path on the RIGHT leading to Lower Slaughter. CROSS THE ROAD WITH CARE and take this path. Carry straight on, pass through a gate/stile and continue on the same line to the edge of a field. Cross this to a stile at the edge of woodland.

Go over and follow the path as it curves down through the trees to the edge of a field. Head across towards a gate and pass through paddocks (taking care to shut the gate behind you).

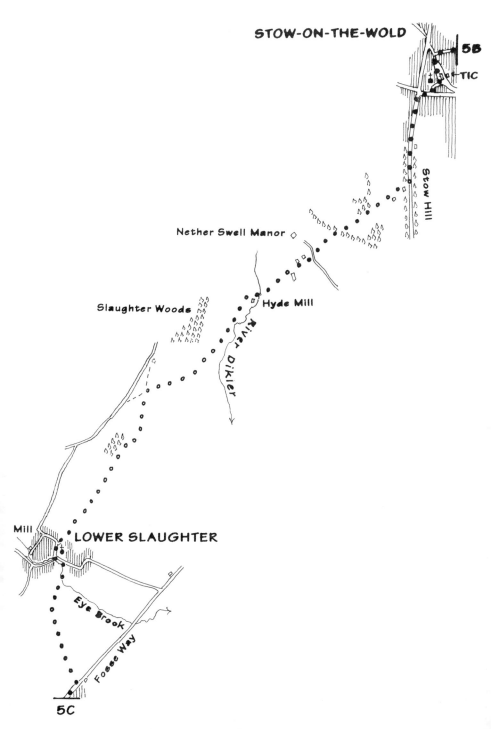

STOW-ON-THE-WOLD

5B

TIC

Stow Hill

Nether Swell Manor

Slaughter Woods

Hyde Mill

River Dikler

Mill

LOWER SLAUGHTER

Eye Brook

Fosse Way

5C

Arrive at a track - cross this and continue forward between a house and stables.

Stay on the same line BUT PLEASE ENSURE THAT YOU FOLLOW THE RIGHT OF WAY when you pass the next house.

Shortly after cross a stile into the field in front. Bear leftish to the TOP LEFT HAND CORNER by a mill. Cross the bridge and then go LEFT around the house. Pass the house on the left and then go RIGHT. Soon after, beyond the stream, turn LEFT into a field.

Walk across the field and then another. In the third field go DIAGONALLY towards the RIGHT where a stile/gate will take you into another field. Take the same diagonal line to another stile/gate. In the next field head for the far side and look for a stile/gate into yet another field.

Enter this and bear RIGHTISH on a DIAGONAL to cut the corner of this field and enter another field. Turn RIGHT and then LEFT to follow the right hand margin of the field towards the houses of LOWER SLAUGHTER. As you approach the end of this field look for a gate/stile on the RIGHT. Go through into the neighbouring field and turn immediately LEFT to head towards the cricket pitch.

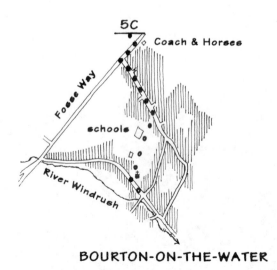

BOURTON-ON-THE-WATER

Go through a gate/stile, go forward and after a few yards enter a path behind the pavilion that will take you onto a drive. Turn RIGHT and then LEFT at the road, which will take you past the church into the heart of the village. Once you reach the river you will be continuing by turning LEFT. (If, however, you want to visit the old mill and its small museum, turn right and follow the river).

After turning left, walk with the river on your right until you meet a path on the RIGHT. Take this and continue until its end at a gate by a meadow. Then bear LEFT to follow the tarmac path across this to the main road. CROSS WITH CARE and turn RIGHT. Then, after a few yards, turn LEFT along the road into BOURTON-on-the-WATER.

Cross over to the other side where practicable and then, after about 400 yards, look for a footpath on the RIGHT that will take you past a school and then the church to bring you to a road. Turn LEFT for the village centre and the River Windrush.

Day 6: Bourton to Prestbury / Cheltenham.

Time: By leaving at 0900 you should arrive in Prestbury at about 1700. Distance (to Prestbury): 13.25 miles.

The longest day! For the first part of the walk you are following a footpath called the WINDRUSH WAY, distinguished by a circle half green and half white.

From the centre of Bourton walk WEST along the main street and follow it out of the village to the main road. CROSS WITH CARE and, just to the right of the bridge, look for a stile/gate that will take you into a meadow with the river on the left.

Carry straight on to enter another field. Keep to the left margin and follow this into woods. Eventually you will come to a track. Do not bear right but follow the track as it bears LEFT down between pretty cottages and comes to a junction. Turn RIGHT and follow the track to Aston Farm. Pass right through the farmyard and then cross a field on the other side. This will bring you to more woodland. Follow this path through the woods for some time.

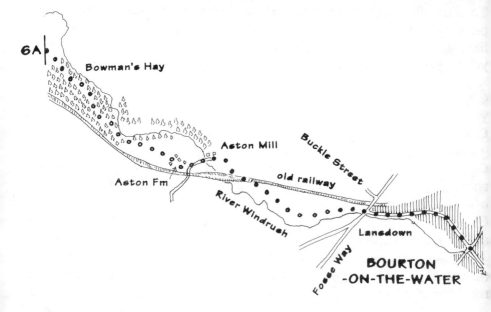

At the end of the woods, emerge into a field through a gate. Cross to the other side, pass through a gate and then bear LEFT through scrubby hillside to gradually descend to rejoin the river. Now you follow the river and cross fields until, a couple of hundred yards to the left of Harford Farm you meet a lane (this last field was the site of a medieval village, which disappeared after the Black Death).

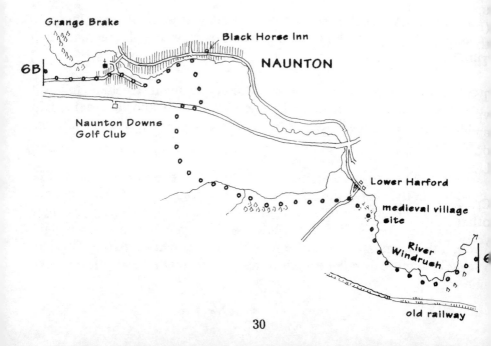

Turn LEFT here for a few yards and then RIGHT into a meadow, with a large pond ahead of you. Turn LEFT and gradually descend to the middle of the field and keep on this line through fields along the bottom of the valley until you reach a stone slab over a small stream on the right.

Cross this, turn directly LEFT and then almost immediately begin to make your way up the slope on the right to the gate at the edge of Naunton Downs Golf Course. You are now leaving the Windrush Way.

Go over the ridge (watching out for golf balls!) until you reach the main road. Turn RIGHT and follow the grass verge for a few yards until, on the other side of the road you see a footpath leading down into NAUNTON. CROSS THE ROAD WITH CARE and follow this path until you meet the river at the bottom.

(Across the road before you is the Black Horse pub; by turning left along the road you will come to a post office and small shop).

Turn LEFT over a stone stile to walk along the left bank of the river and keep going to emerge at a grassy track at the foot of slopes on the left and a gate on the right. Keep straight ahead, however, with the river on the right and on the far bank a handsome, if rather dilapidated, old dovecote.

The grassy track will end at a gate - go through onto a lane between houses until you emerge at the green of Naunton. The walk will continue to the LEFT (but first you might care to turn right for a little way to enjoy the centre of the village with its attractive gardens and river sparkling by the old mill. The church is also worth a visit).

To continue the walk turn LEFT and follow the road as it climbs out of the village. You are now following the Wardens Way, distinguished by a green and white W. After you leave the village behind, look for a stile in the hedge on the RIGHT after about 400 yards. Enter a scrubby meadow and bear LEFT until you come to a stile. Cross this into a field.

Cross the field (there should be a path through the crops) and then at the other side enter another field. Continue on the left margin of this field until you find a gate on the LEFT by a road.

Go through and turn RIGHT. Follow the lane WATCHING OUT FOR TRAFFIC to a junction at the bottom. Cross the road to pass through a gate into a field. Go straight across the field. At the other side leave the field, descend to pass a pond on the left and then enter another field. Go across this towards the church. Pass the church on the right (with its beautiful Norman doorway), the village hall on the left, the old school on the left, and come to a junction. The walk continues to the LEFT but before doing so walk straight on to look at the beautiful village green and, if you wish, visit the Farmers Arms pub for lunch.

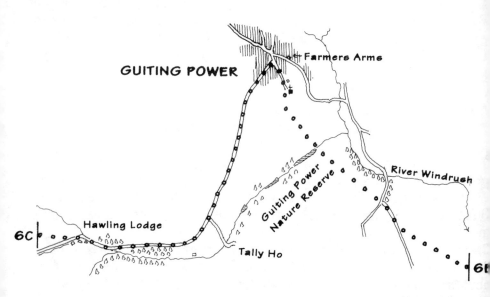

To resume the walk turn LEFT at the junction after the old school (you are now leaving the Wardens Way). Stay on this road for a considerable time (about 1 mile), following the road as it bears right, and eventually you will find yourself in a farmyard (having rejoined the Windrush Way). The road will go quite sharply left and then, just around this corner, look for a track going steeply up to the RIGHT.

Take this and then enter a field; and then keep on this line through a succession of fields, passing to the right of a farmhouse, until you come to a gate at a track. Turn LEFT (leaving the Windrush Way) and continue along here into the village of HAWLING. At the junction turn RIGHT and continue for about 500 yards to the church. Enter the churchyard and, keeping left of the church, continue to a stile at the edge of a field.

Go over the stile and cross the field on the same line (ie diagonally; there may be a sort of fence to guide you) until, on the far side, you come to a road. Cross this to enter another field. KEEP TO THE LEFT MARGIN OF A SUCCESSION OF FIELDS. This will take you to the left of a large new stone house after which you will arrive at the edge of a field in front of you - enter this and then bear LEFT to cross diagonally to a road.

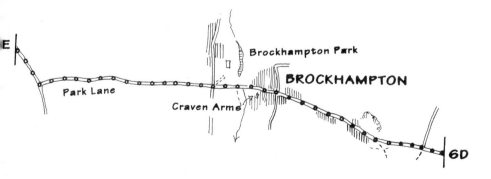

At the road turn RIGHT and continue along this road for some time to the village of BROCKHAMPTON. Pass a number of cottages and a post office and shop as you go.

Eventually come to a small green with a telephone box. Carry straight on, passing a road to the left leading to the Craven Arms pub, until you come to a junction with Brockhampton Park on the right. Cross over and continue on up the road (Park Lane) towards Whitehall. Carry on for some time, until you meet another junction.

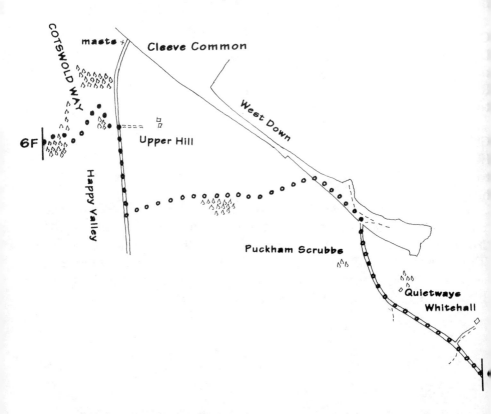

Turn RIGHT here and follow it right to its very end at a sort of parking area at the edge of CLEEVE COMMON. Enter this and bear LEFT. You want to keep to the left margin of this stretch of land, although to do this you will have to look for a gate in the fence in front of you. Go through, cross over the earth gallop` (a track for training horses), and return to the left margin of the field. Fairly soon (about 300 yards) look for a gate on the LEFT leading into a field. Enter this and follow a path/track on the same line for some time (about 1200 yards) as it falls and rises, eventually meeting a road.

At the road turn RIGHT. Walk along here for another 1200 yards, as views of Cheltenham open up below you to the left and look for a stile on the LEFT (opposite a track on the right which leads to a farm).

Cross the stile to head for a copse of trees. Just before the trees turn RIGHT. Then turn LEFT around the trees, following the track quite steeply down towards more woodland (ignoring other tracks left and right). Keep to the track, with the woodland to your left, as it bears RIGHT. Very soon it is joined by a track from the right at a sort of clearing; but keep going as it now bears LEFT and plunges into woodland.

Continue until, just before a house, look for a path through the trees on the LEFT. This will bring you into a farmyard area to the left of the house. Look now for a stile to the right of a barn, which leads into a field - go in and bear RIGHT down the field to a stile/gate among trees. Go through and turn LEFT to another gate/stile. Pass into another field and bear RIGHT.

Go down the field on a diagonal, USING CHELTENHA M'S ONE AND ONLY HIGH OFFICE BLOCK (THE EAGLE STAR BUILDING) AS A GUIDE. Bear towards the left of the field to look for a stile facing you in the hedge about half way down.

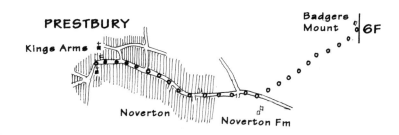

Go over this into another field and head down for a while before curving LEFT around a large bush which will then take you through a gap in a hedge to another field. Go down this field diagonally and the same in the next field, which will bring you to a corner by a lane.

Turn RIGHT and continue to a junction. Keep LEFT to follow the road into Prestbury. At the junction with the main road carry straight on into the heart of Prestbury. From here you may, using the map of Cheltenham, walk back to the hotel or, if you have had enough, call for a taxi, perhaps from the King's Arms pub (further down on the right), which is open all day.

RECORD OF THE WALK

DATE	CONDITIONS & COMPANIONS . .

RECORD OF THE WALK

DATE	CONDITIONS & COMPANIONS . .

RECORD OF THE WALK

DATE	CONDITIONS & COMPANIONS . .

RECORD OF THE WALK

DATE	CONDITIONS & COMPANIONS . .